GHOSTS OF THE HINDENBURG

Ghosts of the Hindenburg

Walking in the Mist of the World's Most Unsettled Mystery of the Twentieth Century

Richard J. Kimmel
Paranormal Archaeologist and Co-Author

Karen E. Timper
Co-Author
(New Jersey Ghost Organization)

Galde Press, Inc. 2022
Hendersonville NC
www.galdepress.com

Cover Design
Stevie Tombstone

Galde Press, Inc.
PO Box 774
Hendersonville NC 28793
www.galdepress.com

Contents

Dedicated to the crew,
passengers, and families of LZ-129
and
Dedicated to Ellen Betty Kimmel
1937-2018, Wife and Mom.

Explosion of the *Hindenburg* burning on ground

Introduction

On May 6, 1937 the New Jersey town of Lakehurst and the Lakehurst Naval Air Station exploded into the annals of history when the German Airship *Hindenburg* made its final flight on that fateful day. This is the untold story of the Hindenburg Disaster and its haunting connections. Was this an Accident? Planned? Paranormal?, and are the spirits of LZ-129 still walking the disaster site? Do some still linger in the Infamous Hanger No.1 and in the streets of Lakehurst New Jersey?

In the opinion of this author this was the beginning of the end for Nazi Germany. The explosion in the tail section of the Hindenburg with fire surrounding the swastikas painted on its tail fins to the brining in the final days of Berlin ending World War II...Fire to Fire! The readers will have to reach their own conclusions however; this book may settle the mystery of this disaster through psychic intervention and the paranormal.

On the surface Lakehurst appears like a typical municipality, but this is a municipality where the departed, those who have yet to cross over, march the lanes during the dark hours. Many ghostly reports have been conveyed by the people who live here, including my own personal experience on two different occasions investigating the infamous Hanger

No.1 with NJGO—New Jersey Ghost Organization. Some accounts may only hold some truth, but in mine and in many minds the departed souls of Lakehurst are all too real.

Individuals visit Lakehurst Naval Air Station throughout the year from all over the country and yes, even foreign countries to visit the site, museum and haunted hanger one.

On each anniversary of the disaster there is a large memorial gathering at the actual crash site to honor those who passed. This is attended by thousands of people. The interest is definitely there and increasing as each year goes by. I and many associates of mine feel so enthusiastic about this book because it is different than any of the run of the mill accounts that have to date been written on the Hindenburg.

I have not only included some basic facts and information about the Hindenburg, but the twist and main thrust of my book, that the other books do not have, is the paranormal connection.

I have always believed that it is not the size of a book that matters, but the content.

—Richard J. Kimmel
Paranormal Archaeologist and Co-Author

Hindenburg exploding just prior to landing.

Ghostly Treasures—Past, Present, and Future

Lakehurst, New Jersey, is not only the site of a U.S. Naval base but also the site of one of the most well known disasters in the 20th century. On the surface Lakehurst appears like a typical small town municipality but, paranormally speaking, this is a place where the departed, those who have yet to cross over, can be felt marching the lanes during the dark hours of the night. Many ghostly reports have been conveyed by the people who live here; some allege these testimonies may not what they seem, but, in many minds, the departed souls of Lakehurst are still all too real.

Tucked away in a remote corner of Ocean County, New Jersey, this small New Jersey town of Lakehurst walked into the annals of history on May 6, 1937, by being known as the site of the Hindenburg Airship Disaster. Now, being revealed for the first time, was this an accident; was this planned, and if so, is there a paranormal connection? Are the spirits of LZ-129 still walking the disaster site, the infamous Hanger No.1 and the streets of Lakehurst? You will soon discover this for yourself as you read through the chapters.

As the fabric of time quickly fades, so do memories at what seems to be light speed. Today the town of Lakehurst is no different from any other historic U.S. town, with one exception: its past has been cast in time, a time not simply for all to remember but, to cherish.

Being a paranormal archaeologist, a published author of several books on specific aspects of this topic, and having been involved with the paranormal for many years, working with haunted artifacts for many years and participating on many major investigations, I have been able to present reasonably conclusive evidence that there exist two common type of haunting: one involving the interactive or intelligent spirit, the other being residual in nature.

One of the most common misconceptions floating around is the difference between "Spirits" and "Ghosts." A Spirit is that of a human who has passed and chooses to interact with the present. Ghosts are images of the past, that have been commonly termed as residual haunting. This is the latent energy of an event or an action that had taken place during a previous time period at a specific location and the imprint has been recorded. When the conditions are amicable, it is played back, similar to a looped video.

A residual haunting that is not unlike a time capsule; this snapshot back in time is revealing a scene that in retrospect is historical and one that may not be discovered in written history. This type of haunting, when viewing it, may seem a bit frightening at times, but you are in no danger, so, sit back and enjoy the experience.

Among the major differences between a spirit, and the ghost or ghosts you see in residual haunting is that you cannot interact with the residual haunting; you cannot be a participant. Some interactive spirits choose to remain behind for many reasons, while others have not yet realized they have passed on.

Individuals have reported seeing a residual ghost image of the airship itself on stormy evenings in the sky over Lakehurst, as if it were making its way to the landing site. Should this be the case, it would more likely be possible that it would be seen on the actual day of the disaster, Thursday, May 6, 1937. However, keep in mind that May 6 does not always fall on a Thursday and the time to get a possible glimpse of this phenomenon would be on a Thursday evening closest to May 6, at approximately the same time that the Hindenburg was making its way to the airfield.

Should the weather conditions be similar, or not, it may be possible to view this residual, providing you are looking in the area of the sky as indicated on the approach map; North, South, East, West etc. To my knowledge no one has captured a photograph of this residual, but I would not discount the possibility.

With historic events such as the one following, it has been alleged, that especially on summer evenings during thunderstorm activity many unusual happenings take place in the vicinity of the crash and in the area of Hangar No.1 and are reported by many who visit the site to be haunted.

rr

Captain Pruss

Commanding Captain of the LZ 129 Hindenburg, survived the crash but sustained burns and required surgery the rest of his life.

Up to the day he died, in 1960, he believed the Hindenburg was destroyed by a bomb.

He was 69 years old.

BEGINNING OUR JOURNEY

Brief Historical Timeline of the Hindenburg

March 26, 1936: Germany's 804-foot Hindenburg launched; begins propaganda tour.

May 6, 1936: Hindenburg inaugurates first scheduled passenger air service between Europe and the United States.

August 1936: Hindenburg appears at the Berlin Olympics' opening ceremonies.

May 3, 1937: Hindenburg departs Frankfurt on final voyage...and of course, we know that the disaster finally occurred on May 6th, 1937, at the Lakehurst Naval Air Station (NAS) in Lakehurst, New Jersey.

The history of NAS began as a munitions-testing site for the Imperial Russian Army in 1916. It was then acquired by the United States Army as Camp Kendrick during World War I. The United States Navy purchased the property in 1921 for use as an airship station and renamed it Naval Air

Station Lakehurst. The Navy's lighter-than-air program was conducted at Lakehurst through the 1930s.

The average trip time between Germany and Lakehurst was about 60 hours (or about two-and-a-half days).

The ship left the Frankfurt airfield at 7:16 PM and flew over Cologne, and then crossed the Netherlands before following the English Channel past the chalky cliffs of Beachy Head in southern England. Then it headed out over the Atlantic shortly after 2:00 AM the next day.

The Hindenburg followed a northern track across the ocean passing the southern tip of Greenland and crossing the North American coast at Newfoundland. Headwinds delayed the airship's passage across the Atlantic, and the Lakehurst arrival, which had been scheduled for 6:00 AM on May 6th, was postponed to 6:00 PM.

By noon on May 6th the ship had reached Boston, and by 3:00 PM Hindenburg was over the skyscrapers of Manhattan in New York City. The ship flew south from New York and arrived at the Naval Air Station at Lakehurst, New Jersey at around 4:15 PM, but the poor weather conditions at the field concerned the Hindenburg's commander, Captain Max Pruss, and also Lakehurst's commanding officer, Charles Rosendahl, who sent a message to the ship recommending a delay in landing until conditions improved.

Captain Pruss departed the Lakehurst area and took his ship over the beaches and coast of New Jersey to wait out the storm. By 6:00 PM conditions had improved; at 6:12 PM Rosendahl sent Pruss a message relaying temperature, pressure, visibility, and winds which Rosendahl considered suitable for landing.

At 6:22 PM Rosendahl radioed Pruss, "Recommend landing now," and at 7:08 PM Rosendahl sent a message to the ship strongly recommending the "earliest possible landing."

The Landing Approach

The Hindenburg approached the field at Lakehurst from the southwest shortly after 7:00 PM at an altitude of approximately 600 feet.

As the wind was from the east, after passing over the field to observe conditions on the ground, Captain Pruss initiated a wide left turn to fly a descending oval pattern around the north and west of the field, to line up for a landing into the wind to the east.

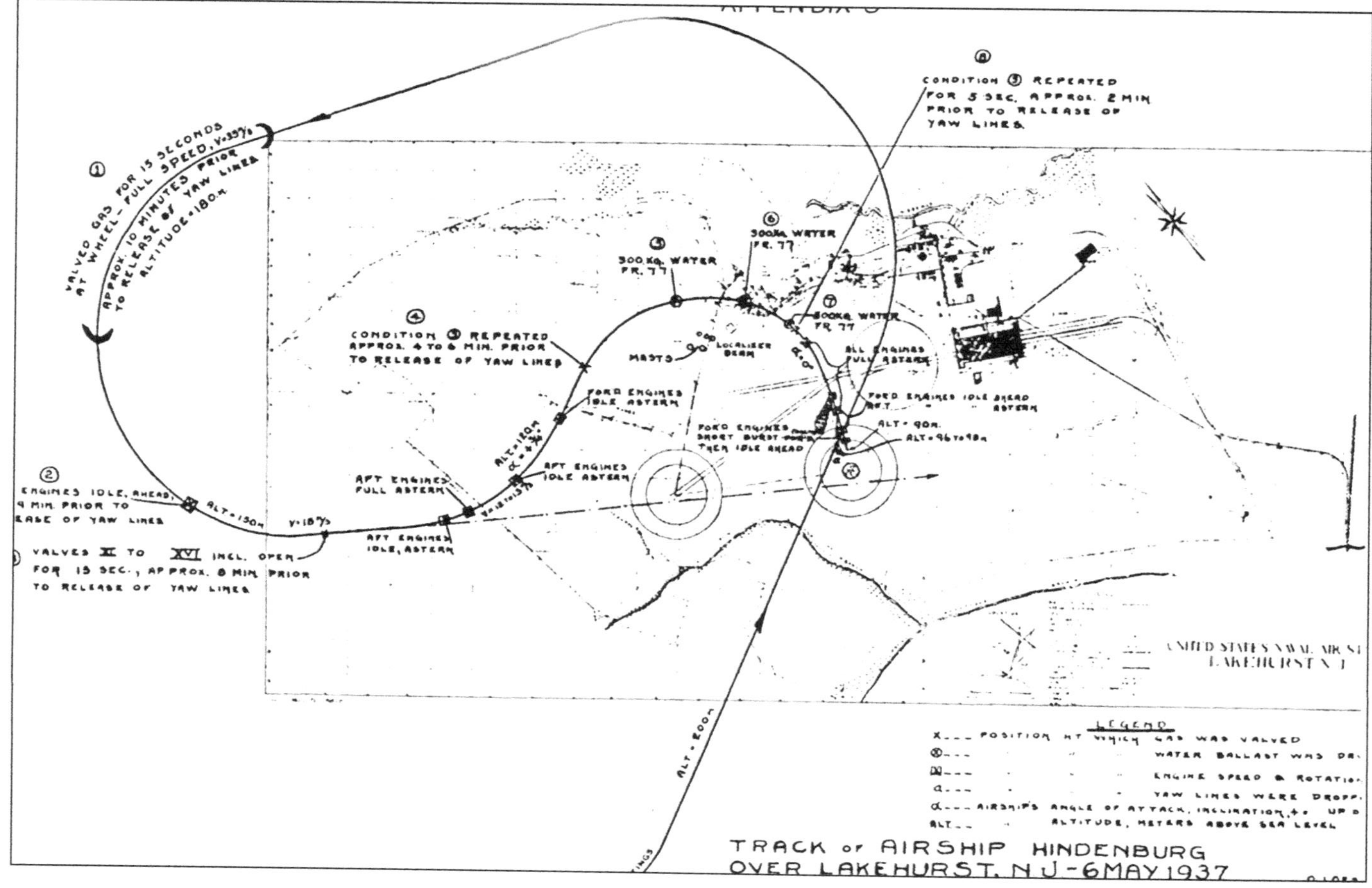
① VALVED GAS FOR 15 SECONDS AT WHEEL - FULL SPEED
APPROX. 10 MINUTES PRIOR TO RELEASE OF YAW LINES
ALTITUDE = 180m
⑧ CONDITION ③ REPEATED FOR 5 SEC. APPROX. 2 MIN PRIOR TO RELEASE OF YAW LINES.
④ CONDITION ③ REPEATED APPROX. 4 TO 6 MIN. PRIOR TO RELEASE OF YAW LINES
⑤ 300 KG. WATER FR. 77
⑥ 300KG. WATER FR. 77
⑦ 300KG. WATER FR. 77
MASTS
LOCALIZER BEAM
ALL ENGINES FULL ASTERN
FORD ENGINES IDLE ASTERN
FORD ENGINES IDLE AHEAD
FORD ENGINES SHORT BURST THEN IDLE AHEAD
ALT = 90m
AFT ENGINES IDLE ASTERN
AFT ENGINES FULL ASTERN
AFT ENGINES IDLE, ASTERN
② ENGINES IDLE, AHEAD, 4 MIN. PRIOR TO RELEASE OF YAW LINES
ALT = 150m
VALVES XI TO XVI INCL. OPEN FOR 15 SEC., APPROX. 8 MIN PRIOR TO RELEASE OF YAW LINES
ALT = 200m
UNITED STATES NAVAL AIR ST LAKEHURST N.J.
LEGEND
X --- POSITION AT WHICH GAS WAS VALVED
ALT --- ALTITUDE, METERS ABOVE SEA LEVEL
TRACK OF AIRSHIP HINDENBURG
OVER LAKEHURST, N.J - 6 MAY 1937

Chapter One

FIRE to FIRE

Could this event have been an omen, the true "Beginning of the End" for Germany's Third Reich? Could American involvement with Germany in the Second World War have actually begun, yet undeclared, back on May 6, 1937 with this unprecedented disaster?

Early on sabotage was considered by some theorists, (including Hugo Eckener, formerly the head of the Zeppelin company; Charles Rosenthal, commander of the Lakehurst Naval Air Station at the time of the disaster; and Max Pruss, the commander of the Hindenburg.

Was this event a deviously planned event from behind closed doors by the hierarchy of the Hitler regime? The answers to these, and other, questions may elude the world forever, at least the world as we know it. Simply, the truth may have been taken to the grave with the eventual death of Adolf Hitler and others who may have been involved in possibly staging this event. But have the answers eluded the paranormal world? Was this a prelude to war?

This untold story of the Hindenburg Disaster may reopen the door to the most catastrophic event of the twentieth century.

From the paranormal perspective, the spirits of the Hindenburg are talking. All we have to do is to stop for a moment and consider the information that may be the initial step in laying this subject to rest.

Many books have been written about the Hindenburg disaster, the details, and the aftermath. Many attempts have been made to connect all of the dots in this mystery; except for one!

This lone dot may hold the key to what actually happened on that fateful day in May 6, 1937. I have provided a simple accounting of the Hindenburg's flight on that day to show the scene; not to rehash the physical disaster itself. If I were to do this it would simply parrot most of what we already know. It's what we don't know that may change the historical outlook.

Most traumatic disasters leave paranormal footprints, the seeds if you will, that will lead us to the known information but, more importantly, information that has previously not been known—the final missing dot!

There are varying opinions, fictional accounts, folklore, and yes, truth, as it was known to be at the time. I believed that there was the need to revisit this traumatic event, that a fresh approach to the past was necessary.

My approach had to be unique and in order to add credence to the many interesting situations. Psychic intervention would be a necessary factor.

I developed a simple investigative process over the years in dealing with the paranormal. Take what is known, include psychic intervention, confirm what has already been known and, more importantly, gain information that has previously not been known. The gathering of physical evidence is equally important to this process, although not always possible and perhaps questionable.

There are times when very clear, vivid, images will come to a psychic. However, most often a psychic will pick up little pieces of information, like a jigsaw puzzle. An attempt must be made to link these pieces together to form the entire picture. There will be times when a specific piece may seem not to fit; until further research indicates that the piece somehow fits into the puzzle. It then becomes part of the picture; possibly it may even be the missing link that helps form a cohesive conclusion regarding that which had taken place.

During psychic interventions, there will be times that a piece of the paranormal puzzle may seem not to fit—even after exhaustive research. This is simply a stray piece of information, possibly from another interactive human spirit in an attempt to interject a communication. It could be an unrelated residual haunting, one that had manifested from a completely unrelated part of the past. Sorting this out may be difficult for the paranormal investigator. However, more often than not, in the future the stray piece may fit—connecting the final dot.

The irony of this chapter in history is that the Hindenburg Disaster began with fire and the Third Reich ended in fire.

Chapter Two

Hallowed Ground

Are some spirits of LZ129 still lingering, not ready to cross over, walking the disaster area? My answer is unequivocally, "yes!" I base this on personal experiences encountered at the Naval Air Stations disaster site and in the infamous haunted hangar No.1.

My first experience took place several years ago when I participated in an investigation at NAS with the New Jersey Ghost Organization. Encounters, both past and present, have taken three forms of haunting; interactive, residual and a combination of both. The paranormal enthusiast could not ask for a better setting that is worthy of continued investigation

Some of the encounters may be considered as being confirmed, while others may not. With some evidence, we simply have the word of the individuals who had the experience.

Where plausible, I will interject psychic reactions.

Every year, on the occasion of the disaster's anniversary, individuals who gather at the crash site cannot help but to come away saying that while they were there, they had a strange feeling of not being alone. It seems that some visitors from the past are still there or have simply returned to pay their "spirited" respects!

The Memorial of the Landing Area

Walking the Streets of Lakehurst

Some of what I uncovered was simply either a story, some previously folklore. The situations that do not fall into these two categories may give you cause to open your minds to the paranormal. I respect the skepticism that some readers may have about the paranormal, the grey area of the unknown or that we think is not known, until they experience it for themselves.

I have always believed that a skeptic only needs that missing dot to bring them to this realization—that when we leave this realm we will emerge into another realm. I prefer to believe that a skeptic needs only a slight nudge to fully realize, not just the possibility that the paranormal exists in our daily lives but, the probability.

Revisiting the past from a paranormal view, I needed as much fresh information as I could possibly gather beforehand. I decided that the first and best place to visit was the Lakehurst Historical Society Museum.

I encountered many interesting people along the way, their stories, encounters and opinions, as will be presented in chapter seven.

The Welcome Sign to Lakehurst at the Base Entrance

Chapter Three

LAKEHURST'S "SILVER GHOST"

Several years ago I heard that on stormy, electricity in the air, spring evenings, especially around May 6, and approximately the time of the disaster of 1937, the whirring sound from the engines of the Hindenburg could be heard on its fateful approach. Between flashes of lightning and rumbling thunder people reported seeing a faint eerie image of, what I've dubbed as, the "Silver Ghost." Could this be fact or fiction? My belief is that this scenario would be possible. This and the many instances of paranormal intervention, may help you reach a positive conclusion.

I find myself peering into the evening sky in the direction of Lakehurst on stormy evenings from my home in nearby Whiting, within the time frame of the disaster, entertaining the hope that I may catch a glimpse of the "Silver Ghost," as a residual effect.

The Airship

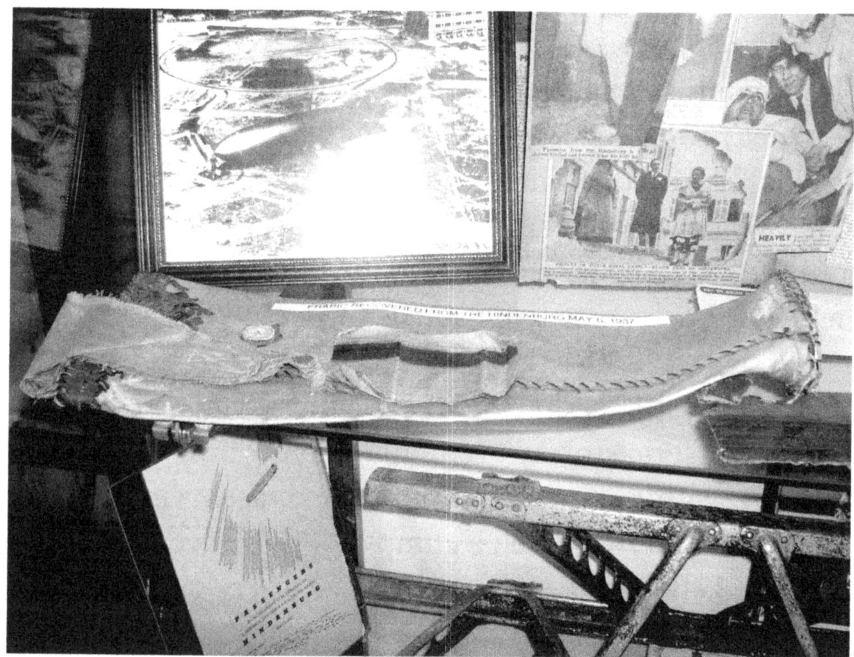

Fabric Recovered

Chapter Four

VOICES FROM THE PAST

A Slice Out of Time

Historic events such as the one following, easily foster the birth of folklore. It has been alleged that, especially on summer evenings during thunderstorm activity, many unusual happenings are said to take place in the vicinity of the crash and in the area of Hangar No.1 This has been reported by many who visit the site to be haunted.

Beginning Our Journey

The Haunting— As fate would have it, a gentleman, with several of his friends, from Columbus, New Jersey, made an eleventh hour decision to travel to Lakehurst, New Jersey, to witness the scheduled arrival of the Giant Airship LZ129 Hindenburg at 7:25 PM that evening, May 6, 1937.

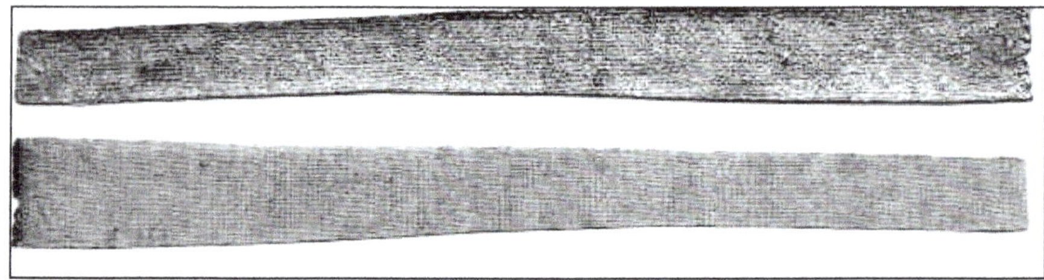

Small charred piece of the outer skin of the Hindenburg

The airship's skin was made of cotton, doped (plasticized lacquer) with a mixture of reflective materials to protect the gas bags within from both ultraviolet and infrared rays.

This is part of our personal collection now.

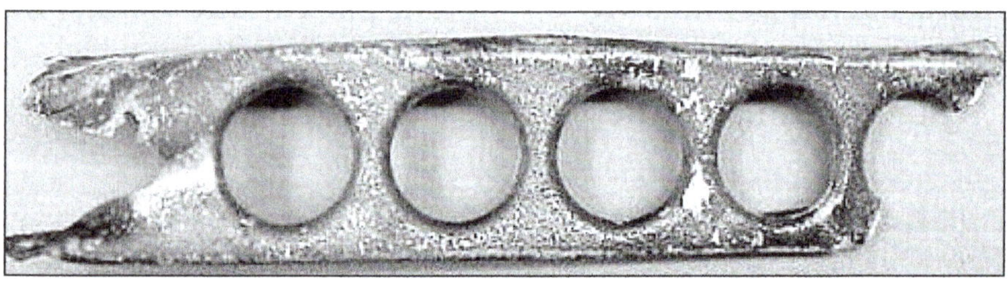

Section of one of the girders from the framework of the Hindenburg

"During the ensuing chaos, tiny pieces of the "skin" (outer covering) of the airship fluttered to the ground, one piece landing near the place where the gentleman from Columbus was standing. While the piece was still aflame, he immediately stepped on it to extinguish the fast-burning flame, as he wanted it as a remembrance of the scene he had just been a witness to. Arriving home, he cut the post card size piece into slivers, for himself and for his friends. One of the skin slivers now resides in my archive.

Every year on the occasion of the disaster's anniversary, individuals who gather at the crash site cannot help but to come away saying that while they were there, they had a strange feeling of not being alone. It seems that some visitors from the past are still there or simply come back to pay their "spirited" respects.

Psychic Reactions

Holding the tiny piece of outer skin in her cupped hands, a New Jersey Ghost O's psychic's first reaction was startling. "My hands felt hot, very hot! A woman's face briefly flashed before me and I could hear sounds of screaming, of running, and a great deal of terror. Very distinct was a voice shouting of the words 'Away the lines.' I could see the letters HIN and I was directed to the top right portion where a fire that is engulfing what appears to be a flying ship began. This is where this piece originated."

I didn't know the location on the giant airship from which the piece had originated. Since this evaluation I have made several visits to Lakehurst and its infamous haunted Hangar No.1.

Extremely haunted is the tarmac area in front of the

famous Hangar No.1 and inside the hangar at the NAS (Naval Air Station) at Lakehurst, New Jersey. Voices have been heard revealing the mass confusion related to the disaster of that infamous evening, May 6,1937, when 36 unsuspecting individuals, returning from an air voyage to Germany, lost their lives in a ball of flame in a matter of a few seconds.

From inside the hangar, at times when no one should be present, the whirring of engines can be heard. At times, a lone, misty figure has been seen lingering on one of the overhead catwalks, near the roofline, and when called to, doesn't reply. On some evenings, near one of the night security lights inside the hangar, a figure can be seen. When security personnel move toward it for a closer look, the figure seems to vanish.

When I had the opportunity to discuss this with another psychic, I was informed that when she had visited this area many years also, visitors were actually permitted in a small building to the right of the crash site. in front of Hangar No.1, that was used as an actual temporary morgue.

Some bodies of the crash victims may have been brought directly into the hangar but soon after, taken to the smaller building. Some of the victims were immediately transported to area hospitals. Thirty-six people had perished in this horrific accident, so it is not surprising that stories emanate of spirits that still haunt the tarmac and the hangar that once housed this magnificent giant of the sky.

Lakehurst Hangar 1 Main Area.

Anomaly captured on film camera. It is considered a "low density" orb. It was not in motion at the time of capture.

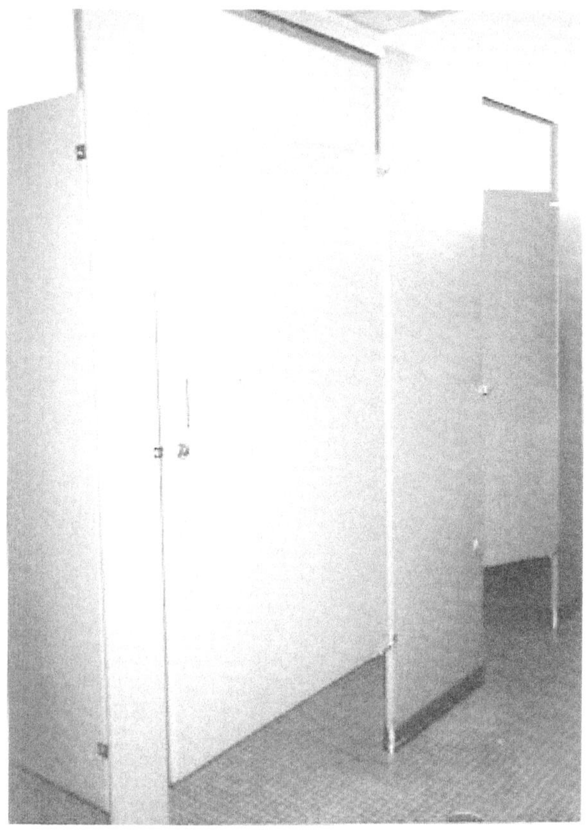

Lakehurst Hangar 1 Bathroom.

Up above the stall door this anomaly was captured on film (not digital). It is an "orb" and is of low density. It is hard to tell if it is three dimensional and not "in motion" at the time of capture. When only one or two are captured it is usually not dust.

Lakehurst Hangar 1 Stairwell.

Lakehurst Hangar 1 stairwell was used as a temporary morgue. This anomaly was captured on film (not digital). It is an "orb" and meets the criteria when evaluating such captures. It is circular, three-dimensional, self-luminous and it is also moving and a very high density. It is a very concentrated form of energy and derived from no source. When they are captured like this it would not be considered dust.

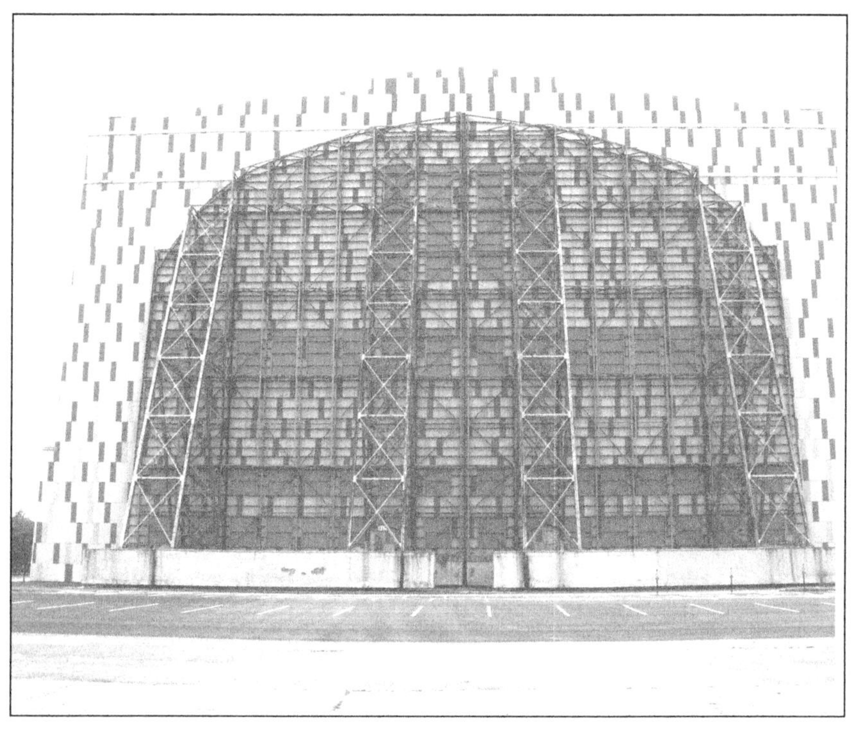

Front view of haunted hangar No. 1

Chapter Five

INFAMOUS HANGAR NO. 1

The Investigation

Before moving to a retirement village in Whiting, New Jersey, I had the opportunity to visit Lakehurst NAS as a part of an investigation with my daughter's group NJGO: New Jersey Ghost Organization. As this was my first visit to the Naval Air Station, I was a bit apprehensive as we made our way toward the area where all this had taken place—walking in the footprints of tragic history.

Never did I think that one day I would be living within a few miles of where this disaster had taken place.

The tarmac area in front of Hangar No. 1 is extremely haunted NAS (Naval Air Station) at Lakehurst, New Jersey. Voices havc been heard revealing the mass confusion related to the disaster of that infamous evening, May 6, 1937.

As a member of the New Jersey Ghost Organization, this investigation and experience proved to be a bit unusual.

Before we had the opportunity to even begin the investigation, we checked our equipment. One of the members had placed their digital camera on one of the crates in the hangar after replacing the batteries. As we were discussing the order of the investigation, the door of the camera's battery compartment mysteriously opened and the batteries were projected about ten feet from the camera, literarily flying through the air. Now, you might be inclined to describe this as a fluke however, given the haunted history of Hangar No.1, this was just the prelude of what was yet to learn.

Chapter Six

"Oh, the Humanity"

Most visitors to Lakehurst proper are embodied with the feeling that they have taken a stroll back in time. All seems to reflect serenity; that is until the sun goes down. I could imagine that for days after the disaster, residents were glued to their radios, listening to the newscasts for the latest information.

Herbert "Herb" Morrison's radio broadcast from the crash scene. Morrison and engineer Charlie Nehlsen had been assigned by station WLS in Chicago to cover the arrival of the airship in New Jersey for delayed broadcast.

Radio network policy in those days forbade the use of recorded material except for sound effects on dramas, and Morrison and Nielsen had no facilities for live broadcast. Still, the results became the prototype for news broadcasting in the war years to follow. The fame of this recording had no effect on network policies, however, and it was not until after the end of World War II that recordings were regularly used.

Below is a blow by blow description as this giant of the sky began desending into eternity. Herbert Morrison, describing the events, as broadcast by WLS radio. The quote of the broadcast is as close to verbatim as possible. Morrison's description began routinely but changed instantly as the airship burst into flames:

"It's practically standing still now they've dropped the ropes out of the nose of the ship and (uh) they've been taken a hold of down on the field by a number of men. It's starting to rain again; it is—the rain had (uh) slacked up a little bit. The back motors of the ship are just holding it (uh) just enough to keep it from— It's burst into flames! It's burst into flames and it's falling it's crashing! Watch it; watch it! Get out of the way, get out of the way! Get this, Charlie; Charlie! Its fire and it's crashing! It's crashing terrible! Oh, my! Get out of the way, please! It's burning and bursting into flames and the— and it's falling on the mooring mast. And all the folks agree that this is terrible; this is the one of the worst catastrophes in the world. [indecipherable] it's flames— Crashing oh! Four or five-hundred feet into the sky and it— it's a terrific crash ladies and gentlemen. It's smoke, and it's in flames now, and the frame is crashing to the ground, not quite to the mooring mast. Oh, the humanity! And all the passengers screaming around here. I told you, it — I can't even talk to people, their friends are on there! Ah! It's— it— it's a— ah! I— I can't talk ladies and gentlemen.

Honest: it's just laying there, mass of smoking wreckage. Ah! And everybody can hardly breathe and talk and the screaming. I— I— I'm sorry. Honest: I— I can hardly breathe. I— I'm going to step inside, where I cannot see it Charlie, that's terrible. Ah, ah— I can't listen, folks; I— I'm gonna have to stop for a minute because [indecipherable] I've lost my voice. This is the worst thing I've ever witnessed."

Herbert Morrison,
American Journalist.

Radio announcer from WLS Radio, Chicago, Illinois. He flew from Chicago, to New Jersey to cover the flight and landing of the Hindenburg, and was still covering it when it crashed.

Chapter Seven

Following in the Footsteps of the Past

Random Comments and Analogies

"I have been working in Hangar No.1 for five years and I have heard voices near the west end doors. I have heard doors slamming and also loud bangs in the hanger several times. The voice is of a lady, I think she is speaking German because I haven't been able to understand her. Several of the other guys that work here have heard noises and voices too."

"I work in Hangar No.1 and have been here for four years. It is very creepy late at night and there are tons of noises. It's so huge it is hard not to hear things. I have had several unexplained things happen, such as dragging metal sounds, opening and closing doors (not due to wind), talking, whispering, and the overall feeling of being watched."

Hindenburg exploding just prior to landing

"The Medical Building about three quarters of a mile away is super creepy. Had a voice answer a question with no one around and witnessed by friend."

"A few shipmates and I attended school there for the Navy. We went in after hearing the stories to find some ghost. That's what we got. We all saw silhouettes of people staring and waving at us, also moving sounds and shadows following us as we walked. We heard a woman scream and almost had a grate pushed on top of me. That place is without question haunted."

"I have been working here (NAS) for thirty-five years. I work on the first floor in Building No.120. Used to work second and third shifts and witnessed and heard many strange things back. The basement served as a second morgue for the victims when the Hindenburg crashed. At times the people down there will not work alone. Is Lakehurst haunted? Most definitely."

"US Navy Hangar #4 at NAS Lakehurst, New Jersey is famously haunted. A Naval Officer was supposedly killed during the disaster of the German Zeppelin *Hindenburg*, then seen wandering around inside the hanger during weekends. I often heard that the Navy officially recognized this fact and closed the hangar during weekends. I was on active duty in the '70s and the USN actually published stories concerning this."

"One staff member was working in the old hospital building at the naval base, now a clinic, had heard a loud crash and when he went to check it out, he saw where a large pamphlet rack had fallen; pamphlets had been scattered all over the floor. The staff member said out loud to no one in particular, 'I didn't make this mess; I'm not cleaning it up; you are.'

The man then went home. The next morning, the rack and its pamphlets were back in their proper place. No one was able to ever explain how they got back that way."

"Lakehurst Naval Mobile Construction Battalion 21—based at Lakehurst, our compound is the supposed burial site of the remains of the Hindenburg which crashed there, there have been many reports of sightings, doors closing, and many other things that can not be explained that have happened there."

These few comments, at the very least, serve as evidence for that which had transpired in the past was definitely prologue to Lakehurst's paranormal events today. They serve the purpose of continuity about circumstances that the average individual believes are unexplainable, skepticism if you will. I have always been a firm believer in keeping an open mind and that a skeptic is simply a closet believer. It mirrors the old adage; you have to see it to believe it.

The proof of the paranormal is in the experiencing of it. The following chapters, based on the firsthand encounters by some residents of Lakehurst, will not simply foster the images of the disaster, but will bring you to the realization of just how thin this paranormal veil is.

Lakehurst's Legacy

According to Merriam Webster, a legacy is "something transmitted from the past."

Indelibly placing the small town of Lakehurst into the forefront of the world, the legacy at hand had its birth on the evening of May 6, 1937 and, so something must take place. When you take into consideration all of the information that I have put forth so far, it transcends into being objective. An extremely fine, almost invisible umbilical cord extends between the two.

Lakehurst is a town that lives and breathes its past, remaining in the minds of all who have had the opportunity to visit, to have worked, or have had duty at the Naval base. What your are about to embark on, is only the beginning of a venture; one that you're destined never to forget!

Hangar No. 1

Chapter Eight

Hangar No.1

An interesting aspect of Hangar No.1 is the air currents high inside the hangar. These are amenable for flying motor-less model aircraft, using only rubber band windup propellers to achieve proper height to pickup the air currents. These planes can remain aloft simply by gliding with the various elevations of the air currents.

The currents are present due to the extreme size and height of the hangar and the model planes can remain aloft for considerable periods of time before gliding to floor level. The interaction between the model planes and the air currents is similar to certain species of birds performing this same feat. Crows are one example.

Hangar No.1 also is home to two museums. One is strictly for the Hindenburg Disaster and the other is mostly for

Entrance of museum inside haunted hangar no. 1

wartime periods.

Should you be planning a trip to visit infamous Hangar No.1 and the crash site, I suggest that you bring along your camera and several sets of batteries, as these can be drained of energy rather quickly due to the extreme amounts of paranormal energy present at both locations. You may also consider bringing a digital voice recorder also with extra batteries.

Should you possess psychic ability, this would be a plus as you would detect this energy immediately at the actual crash site and upon entrance to the hangar. Normally, this extreme energy is also felt at times by some who are not blessed with any psychic ability. This energy can be so intense at times, that it can overwhelm novice ghost hunters, even to experienced paranormal investigators. I have not, that I can recall, felt this form of intense energy in my years as an investigator and Paranormal Archaeologist. This is one of those times where feeling is believing!

Still Paranormally Challenging

In August 2006, I had the opportunity to visit the crash site of the Hindenburg and the infamous Hangar No.1 with the New Jersey Ghost Organization. In the nine years that have passed since that visit absolutely nothing has changed. Hangar No.1 is still as haunted and individuals are experiencing paranormal activity on a regular basis.

I visited there on August 8, 2015 accompanied by my good friend, Kenneth Hawthorn. He is employed at the Naval Base and he had arranged this personal tour. It was déja vu from the first moment that I set foot in Hangar No.1. I had just changed the batteries in my camera and instantly their energy completely drained and the chilling feelings returned.

Ken first took me to see other areas of the base before going to the Hindenburg crash site and the museum in Hangar No.1. During our tour, I was again afforded the opportunity to see parts of the base that are not normally seen by those taking the regular tours conducted by the Navy Lakehurst Historical Society soley of the crash site and hangar.

When I visited Hangar No.1 with NJGO nine years previously the area was extremely "hot" then, paranormally speaking. Psychics visually saw spirit images from days gone by and heard voices from the long departed; not just from that day of disaster on May 6, 1937, but some from years since who met their fate in the hangar or in the immediate area. I believe that none of the team escaped chills running up and down their spinesthat day. I know that I will never forget those experiences either.

Lakehurst Hangar No. 1 Catwalk

One of the catwalks in the hangar. This one is where workers have seen a Navy officer (in spirit) walking.

Staff members of the Lakehurst Historical Society

Lakehurst Hangar No. 1

Another view of the interior of the hangar.

Lakehurst Hangar No. 1 Museum

Museum photographs of the Hindenburg on display.

Lakehurst Hangar No. 1 Museum

Replicas of blimps and more hang from the ceiling.

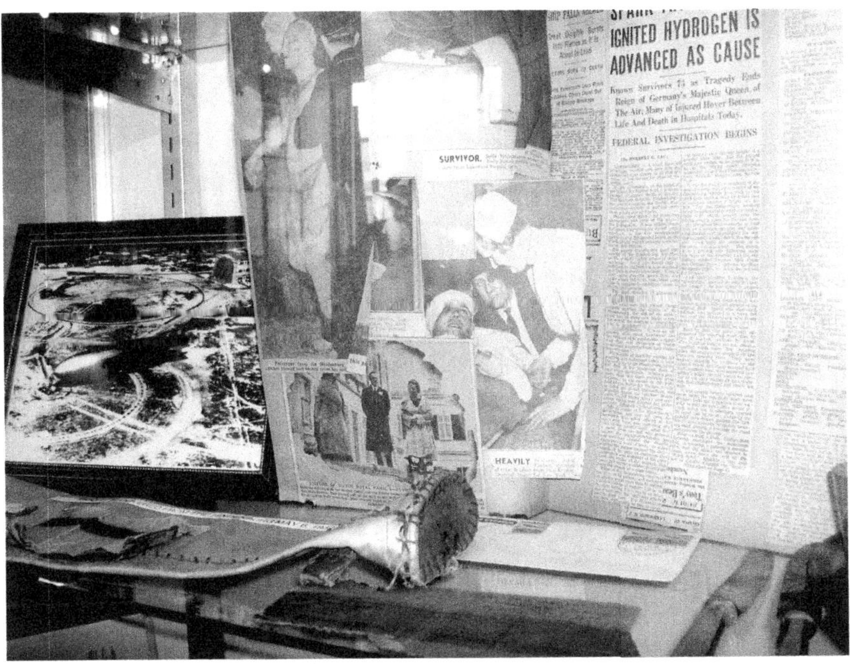

Museum Display.

News photos and articles from the crash of the Hindenburg.

News of the Zep Deaths

Lakehurst Hangar No. 1 Museum.

Girder section from Hindenburg and a close up of a piece of mail that was aboard the airship.

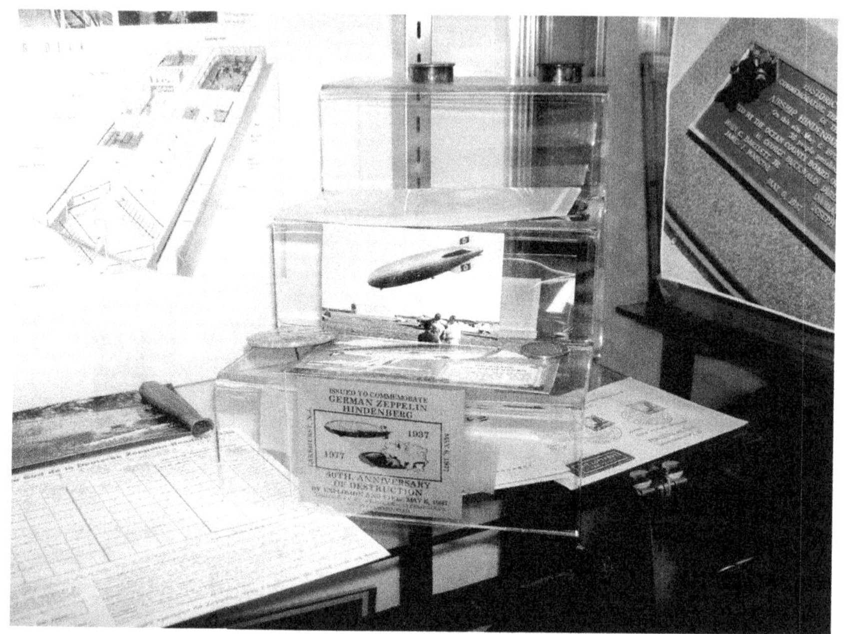

Lakehurst Hangar No. 1 Museum

More ot the Hindenburg-issued items to commemorate the 40th anniversay of the destruction of the Hindenburg.

All museum photos credit to Richard Kimmel.

All orb photos credit to Karen Timper.

HISTORIC LANDMARK
COMMEMORATING THE 50TH ANNIVERSARY
OF THE
AIRSHIP HINDENBURG DISASTER
On this site - May 6 1937 - 7:25 P.M.
36 people perished
DONATED BY THE OCEAN COUNTY BOARD OF CHOSEN FREEHOLDERS
H. GEORGE BUCKWALD, DIRECTOR
JOHN C. BARTLETT, JR.
DAMIAN G. MURRAY
JAMES J. MANCINI
JOSEPH H. VICARI
MAY 6, 1987

Chapter Nine

Passenger and Crew List

Historic events such as the one following, easily fosters the birth of folklore. It has been alleged that, especially on summer evenings during thunderstorm activity, many unusual happenings take place in the vicinity of the crash and in the area of Hangar No.1 and are reported by many who visit the site to be haunted.

As fate would have it, a gentleman, with several of his friends, from Columbus Jersey made an eleventh hour decision to travel to Lakehurst, New Jersey, to be on hand for the scheduled arrival of the Giant Airship LZ129 Hindenburg at 7:25 PM that evening, May 6, 1937.

Barely arriving on time, seeing the giant airship already visible in the stormy sky over Lakehurst, the men rushed to where most of the spectators gathered. Working their way through the crowd, chaos began as the night sky turned red, people began running from the tremendous flash of the explosion, the Hindenburg was being consumed in flame and the aluminum structure was beginning to crumble under the tremendous heat being generated, as the giant of the sky crashed to the ground.

Passenger and Crew List
Below is the list as we know it.
(**asterisk denotes "killed as result of the accident").

13 Passengers
22 Crewmen
One Civilian Ground Crew Member
(Alan Hagaman of Lakehurst, New Jersey)

Ship's Officers, Airship LZ-129 Hindenburg
Captain Ernst Lehmann, Director of Flight Operations, Deutsche Zeppelin Reederei**
Captain Max Pruss, Commanding Officer
Captain Anton Wittemann
Captain Albert Sammt
Captain Heinrich Bauer
Walter Ziegler, Watch Officer
Max Zabel, Navigator
Christian Nielsen, Navigator
Franz Herzog, Navigator
Kurt Bauer, Navigator
Willy Speck, Chief Radio Officer**
Herbert Dowe, Radio Officer
Franz Eichelmann, Radio Officer**
Egon Schweikart, Radio Officer
Rudolf Sauter, Chief Engineer
Eugen Schaubel, Engineering Officer
Wilhelm Dimmler, Engineering Officer**

ELEVATORMEN
Ludwig Felber**
Ernst Huchel**
Eduard Boetius

HELMSMEN
Alfred Bernhard**
Helmut Lau
Kurt Schönherr

RIGGERS
Ludwig Knorr, Chief Rigger**
Hans Freund
Erich Spehl**

STEWARDESS
Emilie Imhoff,**

STEWARDS†
Heinrich Kubis, Chief Steward
Wilhelm Balla
Fritz Deeg
Max Henneberg
Severin Klein
Eugen Nunnenmacher
Max Schulze**

SHIP'S DOCTOR†
Dr. Kurt Rudiger,

COOKS
Xaver Maier, Chief Cook
Richard Muller**
Albert Stoffler
Alfred Grozinger
Fritz Flackus**

– Ernst Rudolf Anders, 65, Dresden (tea merchant)**

ELECTRICIANS
Philip Lenz, Chief Electrician
Joseph Leibrecht
Ernst Schlapp**

ENGINE MECHANICS
Walter Bahnholzer**
Eugen Bentele
August Deutschle
Rudy Bialas**
Jonny Doerflein
Adolf Fischer
Albert Holderried**
Richard Kollmer
Robert Moser**
Alois Reisacher**
Theodor Ritter
Raphael Schodler
Willy Scheef**
Josef Schreibmuller**
Wilhelm Steeb
Alfred Stockle**
German Zettel

CABIN BOY
Werner Franz

Werner Franz
Cabin Boy, Age 14.
In charge of serving officers and crew.
AP & Wikipedia

PASSENGERS

– Leonhard Adelt, 56, Dresden, (writer)
– Gertrud Adelt, 36 (Mrs. Leonhard, writer)
– Ernst Rudolf Anders, 65, Dresden (tea merchant)**
– Ferdinand Lammot Belin, 24, Washington D.C. (student)
– Birger Brink, Stockholm (correspondent)**
– Karl Otto Clemens, 28, Bonn, (photographer)
– Hermann Doehner, 50, Mexico City (Pharmaceuticals Importer)**
– Matilda Doehner, 35 (Mrs. Hermann)
– Irene Doehner, 16**
– Walter Doehner, 8
– Werner Doehner, 6
– J. Burtis Dolan, 47, Chicago (Perfume Importer)**
– Edward Douglas, 39, Newark N.J, (Advertising Account Executive)**
– Fritz Erdmann(Colonel, German Luftwaffe)**
– Otto Ernst, 70, Hamburg (Cotton Broker)**
– Else Ernst, 62 (Mrs. Otto)
– Moritz Feibusch, 57, San Francisco (Fancy Goods Importer)**
– George Grant, 63, London (Shipping Line Executive)
– Klaus Hinkelbein, (Lieutenant, German Luftwaffe)
– George Hirschfeld, 36, Bremen (Cotton Broker)
– Marie Kleemann, 61, Hamburg
– Erich Knoecher, 38, Zeulenroda (Importer)** (Industrial Manufacturing VP)
– Philip Mangone, 57, New York City (Fashion Designer)

– William Leuchtenberg, 61, Larchmont, N.Y. (Industrial Manufacturing VP)
– Philip Mangone, 57, New York City, (Fashion Designer)
– Margaret Mather, 60, Rome (Heiress)
– Nelson Morris, 46, Chicago (Controlling Heir of Meat Packing/Stockyard Inerests)
– Herbert O'Laughlin, 28, Elgin Illinois, (Manufacturing Executive)
– Clifford Osburn, 37, Chicago (International Farm/Industrial Machinery Sales Exec)
– John Pannes, 61, Long Island (American Rep., Hamburg-America Line)**
– Emma Pannes, 60, (Mrs.John)**
– Otto Reichhold, 40, Vienna (Manufacturing Representative)**
– Joseph Spah, 32, Long Island (Acrobat/Stage Entertainer)
– Emil Stoeckel, Frankfurt
– Hans Vinholt, 65, Copenhagen (Retired Banker)
– Rolf von Heidenstamm, Stockholm, (Retired Naval Officer, Industrial Rep.)
– Hans Hugo Witt (Major, German Luftwaffe)

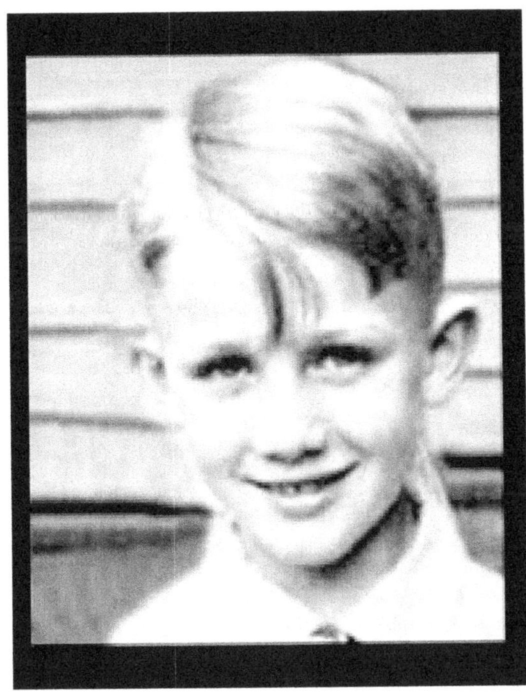

Werner Doehner
Passenger, Age 6
AP & Wikipedia

Werner Doehner
Last known living survivor (passenger).
Died in 2019.
AP & Wikipedia

Werner Franz
Last known surviving crew member.
Died in 2014.
AP & Wikipedia

Chapter Ten

Hindenburg Facts

Even today, the Hindenburg remains the largest aircraft ever flown. Some of the smaller, modern advertising blimps have a total length only slightly larger than the girth of the Hindenburg. If the Hindenburg stood on end it would dwarf the Washington Monument. It could lift 112 tons beyond its own weight, an incredible amount of weight for that time. Passengers enjoyed staterooms with private showers. The dining room served the finest food on blue and gold porcelain place settings. The ship provided the passengers with a spectacular view along its windowed 200-foot-long promenade deck. One restriction the ship had though was about smoking. Because of the hydrogen, smoking was permitted only in a special fireproof room.

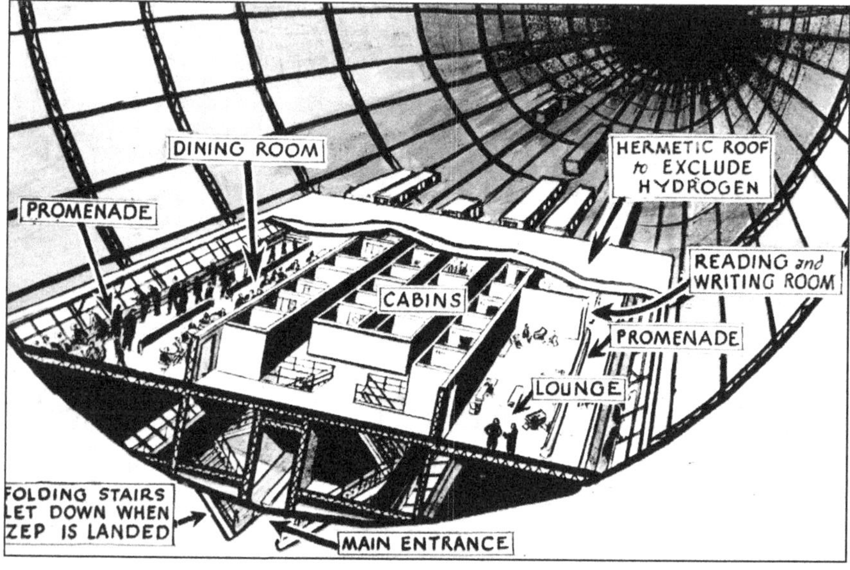

Portion of inside with replica of a ship's flight deck for the purpose of testing aircraft catapults.

Collier's 1956 magazine published a spectacular color reproduction of a painting by artist Doris Lee titled "Catastrophe" depicting passengers parachuting from a Zeppelin bursting into flames above New York. While this painting appears to be inspired by the Hindenburg, which also burst into flames, Lee's painting predates the loss of Hindenburg by more than a year It was on display at the Metropolitan Museum of Art throughout 1936, during the airship's highly acclaimed and successful 1936 season. It was still there when Hindenburg met its fate in 1937.

Facts about the LZ 129 Hindenburg

courtesy of Wikipedia

Type Hindenburg-class airship

Manufacturer Luftschiffbau Zeppelin GmbH

Manufactured 1931–36

First flight March 4, 1936

Owners and operators Deutsche Zeppelin Reederei

In service 1936–37

Flights 63[2]

Fate Destroyed in fire and crash May 6, 1937

LZ 129 Hindenburg (Luftschiff Zeppelin #129; Registration: D-LZ 129) was a large German commercial passenger-carrying rigid airship, the lead ship of the Hindenburg class, the longest class of flying machine and the largest airship by envelope volume.[3] It was designed and built by the Zeppelin Company (Luftschiffbau Zeppelin GmbH) on the shores of Lake Constance in Friedrichshafen and was operated by the German Zeppelin Airline Company (Deutsche Zeppelin-Reederei).

The airship flew from March 1936 until it was destroyed by fire 14 months later on May 6, 1937 while attempting to land at Lakehurst Naval Air Station in Manchester Township, New Jersey, at the end of the first North American transatlantic journey of its second season of service with the loss of 36 lives. This was the last of the great airship disasters; it was preceded by the crashes of the British R38 in 1921 (44 dead), the US airship Roma in 1922 (34 dead), the French Dixmude in 1923 (52 dead), the British R101 in 1930 (48 dead), and the US Akron in 1933 (73 dead).

Hindenburg was named after the late Field Marshal Paul von Hindenburg, President of Germany from 1925 until his death in 1934.

Design and development[edit]
Main article: Hindenburg-class airship
The Zeppelin Company had proposed LZ 128 in 1929, after the world flight of the LZ 127 Graf Zeppelin. This ship was to be approximately 776 ft (237 m) long and carry 5,000,000 cu ft (140,000 m3) of hydrogen. Ten Maybach engines were to power five tandem engine cars (a plan from 1930 only showed four). The disaster of the British airship R 101 prompted the Zeppelin Company to reconsider the use of hydrogen, therefore scrapping the LZ 128 in favour of a new airship designed for helium, the LZ 129. Initial plans projected the LZ 129 to have a length of 813.67 feet (248.01 m), but 10 feet was dropped from its tail in order to allow the ship to fit in Lakehurst Hangar No. 1.[4]

Hindenburg had a duralumin structure, incorporating 15 Ferris wheel-like main ring bulkheads along its length, with 16 cotton gas bags fitted between them. The bulkheads were braced to each other by longitudinal girders placed around their circumferences. The airship's outer skin was of cotton doped with a mixture of reflective materials intended to protect the gas bags within from radiation, both ultraviolet (which would damage them) and infrared (which might cause them to overheat). The gas cells were made by a new method pioneered by Goodyear using multiple layers of gelatinized latex rather than the previous goldbeater's skins. In 1931 the Zeppelin Company purchased 5,000 kg (11,000 lb) of duralumin salvaged from the wreckage of the October 1930 crash of the British airship R101.[5]

Dining Room

The lounge had the world map painted on the wall

Hindenburg's interior furnishings were designed by Fritz August Breuhaus, whose design experience included Pullman coaches, ocean liners, and warships of the German Navy.

The upper "A" Deck contained small passenger quarters in the middle flanked by large public rooms: a dining room to port and a lounge and writing room to starboard. Paintings on the dining room walls portrayed the Graf Zeppelin's trips to South America. A stylized world map covered the wall of the lounge. Long slanted windows ran the length of both decks. The passengers were expected to spend most of their time in the public areas, rather than their cramped cabins.

The lower "B" Deck contained washrooms, a mess hall for the crew, and a smoking lounge. Harold G. Dick, an American representative from the Goodyear Zeppelin Company,[8] recalled “The only entrance to the smoking room, which was pressurized to prevent the admission of any leaking hydrogen, was via the bar, which had a swiveling air lock door, and all departing passengers were scrutinized by the bar steward to make sure they were not carrying out a lit cigarette or pipe.”

Use of hydrogen instead of helium

Helium was initially selected for the lifting gas because it was the safest to use in airships, as it is not flammable. One proposed measure to save helium was to make double-gas cells for 14 of the 16 gas cells; an inner hydrogen cell would be protected by an outer cell filled with helium, with vertical ducting to the dorsal area of the envelope to permit separate filling and venting of the inner hydrogen cells. At the time, however, helium was also relatively rare and extremely expensive as the gas was available in industrial quantities only from distillation plants at certain oil fields in the United States. Hydrogen, by comparison, could be cheaply produced by any industrialized nation and being lighter than helium also provided more lift. Because of its expense and rarity, American rigid airships using helium were forced to conserve the gas at all costs and this hampered their operation.[13]

Despite a U.S. ban on the export of helium under the Helium Control Act of 1927,[14] the Germans designed the airship to use the far safer gas in the belief that they could convince the US government to license its export. When the designers learned that the National Munitions Control Board would refuse to lift the export ban, they were forced to re-engineer Hindenburg to use hydrogen for lift.[11] Despite the danger of using flammable hydrogen, no alternative lighter-than-air gases could provide sufficient lift. One beneficial side effect of employing hydrogen was that more passenger cabins could be added. The Germans' long history of flying hydrogen-filled passenger airships without a single injury or fatality engendered a widely held belief they had mastered the safe use of hydrogen. Hindenburg's first season performance appeared to demonstrate this.[citation needed]

Five years after construction began in 1931, Hindenburg made its maiden test flight from the Zeppelin dockyards at Friedrichshafen on March 4, 1936, with 87 passengers and crew aboard. These included the Zeppelin Company chairman, Dr. Hugo Eckener, as commander, former World War I Zeppelin commander Lt. Col. Joachim Breithaupt representing the German Air Ministry, the Zeppelin company's eight airship captains, 47 other crew members, and 30 dockyard employees who flew as passengers.[15] Harold G. Dick was the only non-Luftschiffbau representative aboard. Although the name Hindenburg had been quietly selected by Eckener over a year earlier, only the airship's formal registration number (D-LZ129) and the five Olympic rings (promoting the 1936 Summer Olympics to be held in Berlin that August) were displayed on the hull during its trial flights.

As the airship passed over Munich on its second trial flight the next afternoon, the city's Lord Mayor, Karl Fiehler, asked Eckener by radio the LZ129's name, to which he replied "Hindenburg." On March 23, Hindenburg made its first passenger and mail flight, carrying 80 reporters from Friedrichshafen to Löwenthal. The ship flew over Lake Constance with Graf Zeppelin.

Hindenburg's logotype (modern recreation)
The name Hindenburg lettered in 6-foot-high (1.8 m) red Fraktur script (designed by Berlin advertiser Georg Wagner) was added to its hull three weeks later before the Deutschlandfahrt on March 26, no formal

naming ceremony for the airship was ever held.

Flag of the Deutsche Zeppelin-Reederei GmbH
The airship was operated commercially by the Deutsche Zeppelin Reederei (DZR) GmbH, which had been established by Hermann Göring in March 1935 to increase Nazi influence over airship operations. The DZR was jointly owned by the Luftschiffbau Zeppelin (the airship's builder), the Reichsluftfahrtministerium (German Air Ministry), and Deutsche Lufthansa A.G. (Germany's national airline at that time), and also operated the LZ 127 Graf Zeppelin during its last two years of commercial service to South America from 1935 to 1937. Hindenburg and its sister ship, the LZ 130 Graf Zeppelin II (launched in September 1938), were the only two airships ever purpose-built for regular commercial transatlantic passenger operations, although the latter never entered passenger service before being scrapped in 1940.

After a total of six flights made over a three-week period from the Zeppelin dockyards where the airship had been built, Hindenburg was ready for its formal public debut with a 4,100-mile (6,598 km) propaganda flight around Germany (Die Deutschlandfahrt) made jointly with the Graf Zeppelin from March 26 to 29. This was to be followed by its first commercial passenger flight, a four-day transatlantic voyage to Rio de Janeiro that departed from the Friedrichshafen Airport in nearby Löwenthal on March 31. After again departing from Löwenthal on 6 May on its first of ten round trips to North America made in 1936, all Hindenburg's subsequent transatlantic flights to both North and South America originated at the airport at Frankfurt am Main.

March 29, 1936 plebiscite ballot
Although designed and built for commercial transatlantic passenger, air freight, and mail service, at the behest of the Reich Ministry for Public Enlightenment and Propaganda (Reichsministerium für Volksaufklärung und Propaganda or Propagandaministerium), Hindenburg was first pressed into use by the Air Ministry (its DLZ co-operator) as a vehicle for the delivery of Nazi propaganda. On March 7, 1936, ground forces of the German Reich had entered and occupied the Rhineland,

a region bordering the Netherlands, Luxembourg, Belgium, and France, which had been designated in the 1919 Treaty of Versailles as a de-militarized zone established to provide a buffer between Germany and those neighboring countries.

In order to justify its remilitarization—which was also a violation of the 1925 Locarno Pact—a post hoc plebiscite (or referendum) was quickly called by Hitler for March 29 to "ask the German people" to both ratify the Rhineland's occupation by the German Army, and to approve a single party list composed exclusively of Nazi candidates to sit in the new Reichstag. The Hindenburg and the Graf Zeppelin were designated by the government as a key part of the process.[27]

As a public relations ploy, Propaganda Minister Joseph Goebbels demanded that the Zeppelin Company make the two airships available to fly "in tandem" around Germany over the four-day period prior to the voting with a joint departure from Löwenthal on the morning of March 26.While gusty wind conditions that morning would prove to make the process of safely launching the new airship a difficult one, Hindenburg's commander, Captain Ernst Lehmann, was determined to impress the politicians, Nazi party officials, and press present at the airfield with an "on time" departure and thus proceeded with its launch despite the adverse conditions. As the massive airship began to rise under full engine power it was caught by a 35-degree crosswind gust, causing its lower vertical tail fin to strike and be dragged across the ground, resulting in significant damage to the bottom portion of the airfoil and its attached rudder.

Zeppelin Company Chairman Eckener, who had opposed the joint flight both because it politicized the airships and had forced the cancellation of an essential final endurance test for Hindenburg, was furious and rebuked Lehmann.

Graf Zeppelin, which had been hovering above the airfield waiting for Hindenburg to join it, had to start off on the propaganda mission alone while LZ 129 returned to its hangar. There temporary repairs were quickly made to its empennage before joining up with the smaller airship several hours later. As millions of Germans watched from below, the two giants of the sky sailed over Germany for the next four days and three nights, dropping propaganda leaflets, blaring martial music and slogans from large loudspeakers, and broadcasting political speeches from a makeshift radio studio aboard Hindenburg.

First commercial passenger flight

With the completion of voting on the referendum (which the German Government claimed had been approved by a "98.79% 'Yes' vote"), Hindenburg returned to Löwenthal on March 29 to prepare for its first commercial passenger flight, a transatlantic passage to Rio de Janeiro scheduled to depart from there on March 31. Hugo Eckener was not to be the commander of the flight, however, but was instead relegated to being a "supervisor" with no operational control over Hindenburg while Ernst Lehmann had command of the airship. To add insult to injury, Eckener learned from an Associated Press reporter upon Hindenburg's arrival in Rio that Goebbels had also followed through on his month-old threat to decree that Eckener's name would "no longer be mentioned in German newspapers and periodicals" and "no pictures nor articles about him shall be printed." This action was taken because of Eckener's opposition to using Hindenburg and Graf Zeppelin for political purposes during the Deutschlandfahrt, and his "refusal to give a special appeal during the Reichstag election campaign endorsing Chancellor Adolf Hitler and his policies." The existence of the ban was never publicly acknowledged by Goebbels, and it was quietly lifted a month later.

While at Rio, the crew noticed one of the engines had noticeable carbon buildup from being run at low speed during the propaganda flight days earlier. On the return flight from South America, the automatic valve for gas cell 3 stuck open. Gas was transferred from other cells through an inflation line. It was never understood why the valve stuck open, and subsequently the crew only used the hand-operated maneuvering valves for cells 2 and 3. 38 hours after departure, one of the airship's four Daimler-Benz 16-cylinder diesel engines (engine car no. 4, the forward port engine) suffered a wrist pin breakage, damaging the piston and cylinder. Repairs were started immediately and the engine functioned on fifteen cylinders for the remainder of the flight. Four hours after engine 4 failed, engine no. 2 (aft port) was shut down, as one of two bearing cap bolts for the engine failed and the cap fell into the crank case. The cap was removed and the engine was run again, but when the ship was off Cape Juby the second cap broke and the engine was shut down again. The engine was not run again to prevent further damage. With three engines operating at a speed of 62.6 miles per hour (100.7 km/h) and headwinds reported over the English Channel, the crew raised the airship in search of counter-trade winds usually found above 5,000 feet (1,500 m), well beyond the airship's pressure altitude. Unexpectedly, the crew found such a wind at the lower altitude of 3,600 feet (1,100 m) which permitted them to guide the airship safely back to Germany after gaining emergency permission from France to fly a more direct route over the Rhone Valley. The nine-day flight covered 12,756 miles (20,529 km) in 203 hours and 32 minutes of flight time. All four engines were later overhauled and no further problems were encountered on later flights. For the rest of April, Hindenburg remained at its hangar where the engines were overhauled and the lower fin and rudder received a final repair; the ground clearance of the lower rudder was increased from 8 to 14 degrees.

1936 transatlantic season

LZ 129 arrival at NAS Lakehurst, May 9, 1936. USS Los Angeles (ZR-3) is moored upper right.

Hindenburg made 17 round trips across the Atlantic in 1936—its first and only full year of service—with ten trips to the United States and seven to Brazil. The flights were considered demonstrative rather than routine in schedule. The first passenger trip across the North Atlantic left Frankfurt on 6 May with 56 crew and 50 passengers, arriving in Lakehurst on 9 May. As the elevation at Rhein-Main's airfield lies at 364 ft (111 m) above sea level, the airship could lift 13,200 lb (6.0 t) more at takeoff there than it could from Friedrichshafen which was situated at 1,367 ft (417 m). The ten westward trips that season took 53 to 78 hours and eastward took 43 to 61 hours. The last eastward trip of the year left Lakehurst on October 10; the first North Atlantic trip of 1937 ended in the Hindenburg disaster.

In May and June 1936, Hindenburg made surprise visits to England.

In May it was on a flight from America to Germany when it flew low over the West Yorkshire town of Keighley. A parcel was then thrown overboard and landed in the High Street. Two boys, Alfred Butler and Jack Gerrard, retrieved it and found the contents to be a bouquet of carnations, a small silver cross and a letter on official note paper dated May 22, 1936. The letter read: 'To the finder of this letter, please deposit these flowers and cross on the grave of my dear brother, Lt. Franz Schulte, 1 Garde Regt, zu Fuss, POW in Skipton cemetery in Keighley near Leeds. Many thanks for your kindness. John P. Schulte, the first flying priest'.Historian Oliver Denton speculates that the June visit may have had a more sinister purpose: to observe the industrial heartlands of Northern England.

In July 1936, Hindenburg completed a record Atlantic round trip between Frankfurt and Lakehurst in 98 hours and 28 minutes of flight time (52:49 westbound, 45:39 eastbound). Many prominent people were passengers on the Hindenburg including boxer Max Schmeling making his triumphant return to Germany in June 1936 after his world heavyweight title knockout of Joe Louis at Yankee Stadium. In the 1936 season, the airship flew 191,583 miles (308,323 km) and carried 2,798 passengers and 160 tons of freight and mail, encouraging the Luftschiffbau Zeppelin Company to plan the expansion of its airship fleet and transatlantic service.

The airship was said to be so stable a pen or pencil could be balanced on end atop a tablet without falling. Its launches were so smooth that passengers often missed them, believing the airship was still docked to its mooring mast. A one way fare between Germany and the United States was US$400; Hindenburg passengers were affluent, usually entertainers, noted sportsmen, political figures, and leaders of industry.

Hindenburg was used again for propaganda when it flew over the Olympic Stadium in Berlin on August 1 during the opening ceremonies of the 1936 Summer Olympic Games. Shortly before the arrival of Adolf Hitler to declare the Games open, the airship crossed low over the packed stadium while trailing the Olympic flag on a long weighted line suspended from its gondola.On September 14, the ship flew over the annual Nuremberg Rally.

On October 8, 1936, Hindenburg made a 10.5 hour flight (the "Millionaires Flight") over New England carrying 72 wealthy and influential passengers. Winthrop W. Aldrich, Nelson Rockefeller, German and American officials and naval officers, as well as key figures in the aviation industry such as Juan Trippe of Pan American Airways. The ship arrived at Boston by noon and returned to Lakehurst at 5:22 pm before making its final transatlantic flight of the season back to Frankfurt.

During 1936, Hindenburg had a Blüthner aluminium grand piano placed on board in the music salon, though the instrument was removed after the first year to save weight. Over the winter of 1936–37, several alterations were made to the airship's structures. The greater lift capacity allowed nine passenger cabins to be added, eight with two beds and one with four, increasing passenger capacity to 70. These windowed cabins were along the starboard side aft of the previously installed accommodations, and it was anticipated for the LZ 130 to also have these cabins. Additionally, the Olympic rings painted on the hull were removed for the 1937 season.

Hindenburg also had an experimental aircraft hook-on trapeze similar to the one on the U.S. Navy Goodyear-Zeppelin built airships Akron and Macon. This was intended to allow customs officials to be flown out to Hindenburg to process passengers before landing and to retrieve mail from the ship for early delivery. Experimental hook-ons and take-offs, piloted by Ernst Udet, were attempted on March 11 and April 27, 1937, but were not very successful, owing to turbulence around the hook-up trapeze. The loss of the ship ended all prospects of further testing.

Final flight: May 3–6, 1937

Hindenburg on fire
MENU0:00
Live radio broadcast

After making the first South American flight of the 1937 season in late March, Hindenburg left Frankfurt for Lakehurst on the evening of 3 May, on its first scheduled round trip between Europe and North America that season. Although strong headwinds slowed the crossing, the flight had otherwise proceeded routinely as it approached for a landing three days later.

Hindenburg's arrival on 6 May was delayed for several hours to avoid a line of thunderstorms passing over Lakehurst, but around 7:00 pm the airship was cleared for its final approach to the Naval Air Station, which it made at an altitude of 650 ft (200 m) with Captain Max Pruss in command. At 7:21 pm a pair of landing lines were dropped from the nose of the ship and were grabbed hold of by ground handlers. Four minutes later, at 7:25 pm Hindenburg suddenly burst into flames and dropped to the ground in a little over half a minute. Of the 36 passengers and 61 crew aboard, 13 passengers and 22 crew died, as well as one member of the ground crew, a total of 36 lives lost. Herbert Morrison's commentary of the incident became a classic of audio history.

A fire-scorched duralumin Hindenburg cross brace was salvaged from the crash site.

The exact location of the initial fire, its source of ignition, and the source of fuel remain subjects of debate. The cause of the accident has never been determined conclusively, although many hypotheses have been proposed. Sabotage theories notwithstanding, one hypothesis often put forth involves a combination of gas leakage and atmospheric static conditions. Escaping hydrogen gas (in this specific case from incomplete or damaged vents along the top of the vessel and especially near the rear upper tail fin) will typically burn after mixing with air and will explode when mixed with air in the right proportions. This, along with the high static collected from flying within stormy conditions could have combined to ignite the leaking gas and down the airship. In addition, a certain amount of gas may have been inexplicably lost out the top of the vessel for, at the same time, water ballast was noticeably released to slow the rate of descent. The initial explosion would therefore have been the result of the quickening fire reaching the gas bags themselves via the compromised aft-most vent at the vessel's stern.

Another more recent theory involves the airship's outer covering. The silvery cloth covering contained material including cellulose nitrate which is highly flammable. This theory is controversial and has been rejected by other researchers because the outer skin burns too slowly to account for the rapid flame propagation and gaps in the fire correspond with internal gas cell divisions, which wouldn't be visible if the fire spread across the skin first. Hydrogen fires had previously destroyed many other airships.

The duralumin framework of Hindenburg was salvaged and shipped back to Germany. There the scrap was recycled and used in the construction of military aircraft for the Luftwaffe, as were the frames of Graf Zeppelin and Graf Zeppelin II when they were scrapped in 1940.

Additional Photos

Steel girder recovered from the Hindenburg crash.

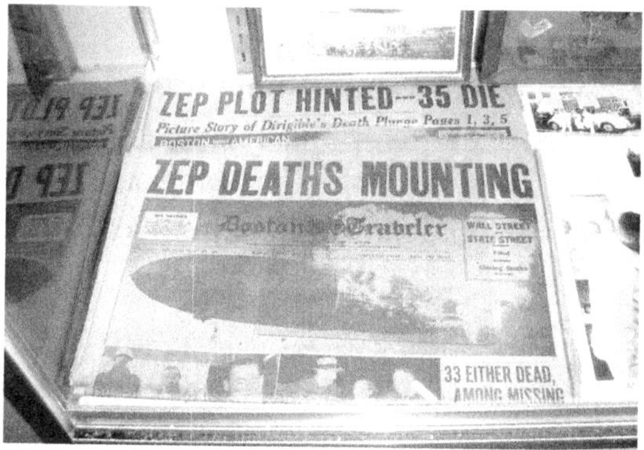

Piece of Hindenburg's outer covering recovered from the crash

Lakehurst Hangar No. 1 Museum
Typical dinnerware used aboard the airship.

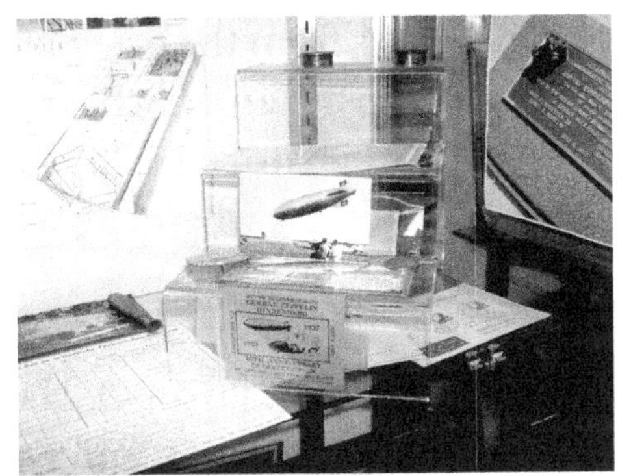

40th Anniversary

Close up view of letter.

1974 Documentary on PBS station. NOVA Season 48-Episode #9 titled "Hindenburg: The New Evidence"

Synonymous with the Titanic, the Hindenburg continues to remain a mystery, never conclusively proven how the Hindenburg, three times the size of a 747 airplane, crashed and burned, or burned and crashed, but the case was reopened with the chance spectator's film that hadn't been seen since 1937.

The original footage was from the original Kodak 8 mm movie camera belonging to a Harold Schenck in which his nephew showed Aviation Historian Dan Grossman, an author and expert on airships, is where the scientific aspect begins.

With the help from Lt. Col. Jason O. Harris, a USAF Reserve Pilot now a commercial pilot, and Dan Grossman they set out to eventually create historically relevant experiments and began the journey with someone who has knowledge of vintage film that authenticated the film and its camera.

They also traveled to Germany to begin a series of tests to see if anything more can be told of the famed airship's fate.

The intent of the airship was to go from Germany to the United States, specifically Lakehurst Naval Air Station in NewJersey with the 97 passengers and crew, re-fuel and return to Germany in a turn around time of approximately foour days. According to the documentary, the goal was to produce and put into service a 40-50 fleet by 1945 as an alternative means of transportation.

Back up a year, 1936. The Hindenburg made many flights and as early as 1929 Graf Zeppelin, the Hindenburg's predecessor flew to Lakehurst without incident.

Going back to the Kodak 8 mm videocamera, all news photographers were shooting the airship's landing from the same angle and unfortunately the same time. No film was capturing the disaster from the moment of ignition—except Mr. Harold Schenck was!

Grossman brings the film in its original box and the camera to ColorLab, a company that restores films for places such as the Library of Congress. The film lasted two minutes in brief moments, not continuously. Because of the aperture wind on the film, you could see the front of the airship and the rear simultaneously when the ship was on fire!

Mr. Schneck was filming near Hangar 1 with a good broadside view, although brief. He had the camera at his side. When he resumed filming he luckily had the camera's switch on and film was rolling, so when he brought the camera up to film it was already filming.

Upon taking a closer look at the footage, it showed the airship was out of trim, which means it was off balance and the tail was showing to be too heavy. The ship could not be kept level as they were about to use the mooring ropes.

They most likely tried to valve off (hydrogen) gas trying to make the ship heavier to counter the rear. They did this several times. They tried dropping water ballast. There may have been a pre-existing leak, which begs the theory of sabotage.

Should have, would have, could have stopped and delay the landing to diagnose the leak and fix the issue, but the officers of the ship chose to continue with the landing because they were twelve hours behind schedule. There was no cockpit recorder, so we do not know for sure what was transpiring.

Harris and Grossman visited the airship museum in Germany. The original intent of these airships' makeup was to use helium gas, which was strictly an American resource and hard to get. Congress enacted laws so you would have to get approval to sell outside of the U.S. The use of hydrogen gas was a risk because it is highly flammable.

The gentlemen proceed to conduct some interesting experiments. There was a question of four minutes from when the mooring ropes were let down to when the ship actually "exploded." Interest was focused on the ropes. The ropes were 14 cm and made of manila hemp. They explained that house electricity flows from one side of the electrical outlet through whatever is plugged into it and back out again to the other side of the outlet, but only flows if it has a path. Take away the path – the flow stops. Think of a living room lamp. If something is broken inside the lamp, the electricity cannot complete its path to lighting up that lamp.

The experiments continued. They created one in a lab

using a sample of similar rope and it was tested to see if it made a spark and how it connected to the hydrogen being used to fly the airship. The rope wasn't pre-charged until it got wet on the ground (due to the fact that it was slightly raining). They applied voltage to both ends of the rope (3000 volts to the top end). With a voltage tester they showed that there is current flowing, even with the dry rope. The voltage increases significantly to 10x more when they wet the rope with water. The ship should have exploded immediately. Why not?

Then they tested the skin covering the Hindenburg. The Celon Dope paint they used to make the shiny silver coat, coupled with the aluminum powder/iron oxide/and cotton made up the final layers of the skin. The Hindenburg had that fabric sewn using grommets and resting on wooden pegs to attach the skin to the metal-framed body. That construction would in theory prevent a charge on the skin from reaching the metal frame. They compare it to a person walking in socks on a carpet and not "quite" touching a light switch, thus giving them a small electrical shock, creating a spark. But the way it's assembled prevents that.

The second part to that experiment they re-created the outer skin and sat electrodes on top of the skin and applied voltage. No spark, no charge to the frame from the skin. They wet the skin (remember it was slightly raining at Lakehurst), plus the ship had just travelled across the ocean. Now they got a spark across the skin and jumped across gaps in the metal frame. It took time for the charge to meet and get strong enough to jump through the gaps.

The last experiment was done to see how much of a

charge the skin can hold based on its surface area (water droplets on the skin) and compared that to atmospheric electricity flowing in the stormy conditions that day. Two hundred and twenty-one seconds, or four minutes. Bingo! The Hindenburg turned into a giant Compacitor. The charge cannot move through the rope, but it moved throughout the skin.

Now here's where and why this disaster still remains a mystery. Some people believe that given consideration between Adolf Hitler's regime, the United States and the world, that sabotage is still on the table, the possibility that the hydrogen leak could have been enhanced on purpose. You decide.

The barometer was dropping and the airship kept shifting. Fire erupted after the mooring lines went down and the Captain immediately said it had to be a bomb and his thoughts went to sabotage. It was found to have hydrogen leaking. The crew reported that they saw an orange glow in one of the gas cells near the tail of the ship and later, observations from the ground also reported the flames. Too much of the ship was destroyed and they had to rely on witnesses. It was never concluded the cause of the spark that possibly ignited hydrogen in one of the gas cells.

So like I said in the conclusion of my notes, it could have been that more hydrogen was leaked than what was necessary to be human error, or hydrogen was leaked on purpose prior to the ship attempting to land at Lakehurst.

Intuitive Information

I (Karen) sat down with our psychic on a late Saturday morning to get his impressions of an artifact I brought to him. He did not know what it was, or how significant it was to a project I was working on. It was the very small sliver of the Hindenburg.

This is what he had to say. He said it was interesting, a metallic-looking piece, like some kind of lining. His first impressions was of being around a plotting, a planning a conspiracy. A covert meeting. He is already getting its spiritual energy. It's part of a larger piece.

He also sees a table in a parlor, a private room. He sees three men. He pauses to perhaps describe it better. He's trying to place the men's clothing. Older clothing, possibly 1800s, possibly describing the decor of wealth. This would be the main man who is responsible for planning this operation. The two other men just visit him.

There is intention here. I ask if this artifact has a knowing. He replies that the cloth (artifact) has absorbed meetings and disagreements. These three men have started down a road in the planning of whatever this is. One of the men was more radical than the others and the disagreement was that this was going too far. That one gentleman wasn't committed to going that far. This planning was at least a week's worth, possibly a couple of months in the planning. This was politically motivated.

Our psychic heard the name "George".

Our psychic was not yet getting an outcome of this. This seems radical, yet looks like they didn't like an individual. He sees a couple of layers here. A family, a husband, and wife. A more stable, happier and peaceful time that this artifact was in an office or study of a male. Someplace where they all met.

The psychic was not sure if this plan was a success. No success feeling.

The trio broke it off, not enough resources. One of the men wanted to do this on his own.

In the background this piece was part of some significant event. Although he is not sure if the piece saw the completion of the planning. The planning was interrupted.

This plot was not positive. There was no rescuing or restoring. Not a lot of people appreciated it. The man thought he was righting a wrong.

The psychic saw fire inside the location of one of the outer walls of where this piece was. He also saw a message of a tavern.

(Karen) asked him if he hears anymore words. He hears a southern voice say U.S.

I ask if he sees colors? A brand? Anything to identify with? He replies, Civil War. Was this fabric manufactured years before? He says lasting a couple of decades, family owned. Metallic in texture. (which he states in the very beginning of this conversation.)

He sees brandy spilled on the piece, sees a brandy snifter, seeing over a fireplace mantle crossed sabers, military officer, not necessarily the man doing the plotting.

I ask what does the artifact (piece) have to say. Does it know what it was used for? He saw the larger piece dropped over something. The artifact was surprised to have been used in the fashion that it is. He is seeing gold/gilding overlay.

He was seeing a lot of sadness. A large population of sadness. He sees nothing outside of the U.S

The piece itself has emotions and has regret. The end result (unknown at this point) was not the same as the intention. The piece feels it didn't support what the outcome would be. Again, expresses regret for unexpected consequences.

I ask the psychic when did he want to know what the artifact is. He replied, "Soon".

I ask him again if he sees colors associated with the artifact. He replies, darker blue cover, hanging cloth thing.

I ask, day or night? He replies daytime.

He sees servants/servers coming in to tidy up. He sees three men.

I ask him if there is anything that really stands out, that the piece says to him? He replies, not at the moment, except for the fact that the atmosphere was a turning point, something that would affect a lot of people.

He repeats the regret the piece (artifact) felt was that it had no control over the end result. He states, "frustration" and "resolution." here was nothing that the piece itself could do.

At this point I told the psychic that this was a small piece of the Hindenburg. He was very humbled to be in the company of such a piece of history.

He explained that this piece came from the bottom of where the gondola would have been, closer to the people (on board).

We end the conversation with the piece thought it would be used strictly for military. The precursor of the energy of the piece was this trip being military, including bombing. Understanding the original intent that the blimp would be used for only military purposes, not what happened in the end.

In my experience as a seasoned paranormal investigator working with some of our most trusted psychics, myself knowing what the artifact was and not disclosing it to our psychic until almost the very end, I could see where the impression had stated.

I wouldn't say that his impressions are up for interpretation, so much as they are what they are. It has never been determined that there was indeed a plot to bring down the

Hindenburg. No one knows for sure how the disaster happened. Only speculations.

Now you cannot shy away from your own interpretations and what was on my mind was that impressions were made as to possibly the fabric used when building the Hindenburg could have been manufactured years before. He sees darker blue, I took that in my mind as Navy. The Hindenburg crashed on a naval base. There was dining aboard the Hindenburg. That could explain brandy, and people serving (staff). It definitely makes for interesting conversation that a psychic sees things that we cannot and examines a piece of something that he or she knows absolutely nothing about.

Author Biographies

KAREN E. TIMPER

Richard's oldest daughter Karen has co-founded and guided New Jersey Ghost Organization on successful investigations of hauntings since 2003 with Richard. Like Richard, Karen was born and raised in New Jersey and is a married mom of two adult children. Karen served as a Hospital Corpsman in the United States Navy in Philadelphia, PA.

Growing up early on in her grandparent's Victorian era house began her journey with the paranormal, but didn't fully understand until her adult years just how much and how long her journey would take her.

Alongside Dad, the journey continues. You can find out more about New Jersey Ghost Organization on Facebook *newjerseyghostorganization.– Photo Credit Sandra Foley, Fashion Haunts Magazine 2018*

RICHARD J. KIMMEL

When not investigating wartime artifacts I am an active member of NJGO; New Jersey Ghost Organization, having become a most recognized, progressive and professional paranormal investigative group in the Garden State since 2003.

Using a pendulum to help detect latent energy, I work very closely with the organization on investigations of local historical buildings and battle sites.

After my military service in the United States Army as a combat photographer, I pursued photography as a profession. Today, when lecturing, I recall my early days as a youth during the chaotic days of the Second World War and always having had an avid interest in military artifacts and historic places.

Beginning with my collection of wartime postal stamps and a few items given to me by returning neighborhood GIs, is what initially laid the ground work, setting me off on a continuous journey down the paranormal road. I recall that I always had strange feelings when handling these artifacts and when visiting historic buildings and battle sites as far back as those early wartime days.

In past years I have written articles for several paranormal publications and in recent years with NJGO, have participated on national television (The Maury Povich Show). I and Karen have been a guest on several internet paranormal radio shows, as well as on local radio and television.

I hope that all who read this and our other books will not simply view them as just a run-of-the-mill book on the paranormal, but will come away with a better understanding of the paranormal, the technical aspects of researching and its connection to artifacts and locations.

From a historical aspect I feel that paranormal archaeology opens the door to information that can be pursued through additional research and in specific cases may change the present historical perspective as we know it. I have always felt that with any type of investigation one should begin with a positive attitude; one of validation as opposed to debunking. Debunking becomes part of the validating process but should not be the main thrust of an investigation.

Artifacts are tangible remnants of the past that offer valuable information about the history of humanity. Without these historical gems, the knowledge of past conflicts and events would be buried in time.

By using psychics I believe, and have proven many times over, that an artifact can provide its own story into a window in time. Thus, it could provide a deeper understanding of why and how our world has been shaped by conflict and events.

Photographs of artifacts are visual treasure maps into the realities of wartime conflicts and of other historical periods. I take artifacts, my military knowledge, and a pendulum to search for latent energy, my belief in psychic ability and combine all of them to test the waters of a new frontier of research. Sometimes, I am shocked by the results of the research. I quivered at times at psychic images of the atrocities of war.

How is it possible for psychics to receive impressions? According to Quantum theory, there are tiny bits of energy that come together and vibrate at a unique level for every person or thing. These 'fingerprints of energy' mark anywhere you have been, anything closely associated to you and even your thoughts have this energy. Psychics sense this energy and are then able to interpret it into images, feelings and sounds.

To those wishing to pursue the paranormal investigation of artifacts, battlefields and other historic locations I would offer the following suggestion to be considered, to remember, that above all, exercise patience; contacts may come when you least expect them.

As an author, researcher and investigator I truly hope that from this work and from our previously authored books, that both the paranormal and militaria collecting communities will realize that the information gained through research, investigation and psychic intervention, may open new and positive avenues for thought. That, in the majority of cases, although not considered a science, paranormal investigative techniques and the positive results obtained may change the present historical perspective, as we know it to be.

To the skeptic I have just one request, to keep an open mind!

Richard J. Kimmel and Tomcat plane at Lakehurst on display.

Karen Timper Hospital Corps-man, circa 1980. Philadelphia Naval Hospital .

Richard Kimmel, U.S. Army. Circa1954. Fort Knox, KY.

Ground crew running

Karen and Richard can be found on Facebook New Jersey Ghost Organization and instagram @newjerseyghost.

Available on Amazon.com or your local Barnes & Noble Books Stores the following titles:
* *WWII Ghosts- Artifacts Can Talk*
* *Ghosts of Central New Jersey-Strange, Bizarre & Deadly*
* *Folklore of the New Jersey Shore - History, the Supernatural & Beyond*

Made in the USA
Middletown, DE
27 June 2023